The Kindness of Stars

Dedication

For Ryu Kurosu Forsythe,
my great-grandson

The Kindness of Stars

by
Fred Cogswell

Borealis Press
Ottawa, Canada
2004

Canadä

*We acknowledge the financial assistance of the
Government of Canada through the Book Publishing Industry
Development Program (BPIDP) for our publishing activities.*

National Library of Canada Cataloguing in Publication Data
Cogswell, Fred, 1917-
    The kindness of stars / Fred Cogswell.

Poems.
ISBN 0-88887-205-4

    I. Title.

PS8555.O3K55 2004   C811'.54   C2003-907015-8

Cover design by Bull's Eye Design, Ottawa
Photograph on back cover by Emma Hutchman

Printed and bound in Canada on acid free paper.

Contents

I

IF OLD PEOPLE IN CANADA

If old people in Canada
Ended themselves by suicide
I have doubts whether their children
Would remember them with pride
And say, "How noble people were
To save us the cost of our care."

Inside our own generation
We gave them toys for family
And they became what they beheld
Forfeiting their heredity.
As for sharing, girls and boys
Have no use for broken toys.

LINES FOR MY EIGHTY-FIFTH BIRTHDAY

My last dog was black, female and Chinese.
Massive-muscled, compact and powerful,
On any walk she had a mighty pull.
So thick her wool was she would never freeze.

She made herself my dog and tried to please
Me, half-blind. Winter roads were slippery.
Lacking exercise, she lay close to me.
Though cats were there she had no time for these.

Children sometimes came, stood too close at hand,
But what they were she did not understand.
Their motions made her make an awful fuss
And kept the situation dangerous.
I took her to the vet without delay.
That's why my birthday was my dog's death-day.

THE BEACH AT NOON

Full-faced to the brisk sea gale, I breathe air
Cold, sharp, and salt as the white-edged waves
And see the same sea-silver on gulls' wings
That slip the driving wind. Above me now
The sun's noon glory hangs, reminding me
There is some brightness that no eyes can bear.

On the bay's other side the cliffs are bare,
Then sudden flower in the lambent air
Rose-red against the double blue of waves
And sky. But even as I watch them now
Their glow already seems less bright to me
Who in this moment feel my lack of wings.

Fixed on this spot even as the wind wings
Up cloud and shape-dissolving rain, I bear
The pain of seeing now a scene I know
I am a part of patterned in the air
With all of air's fragility—cliff, waves,
Sun, sky, gull wings one instant fused in me!

Although the core of consciousness is me,
The power is otherwhere. Outside are wings
Of wind and gull, are sun, cliff, sky, and waves
That, despite my hope and memory, bear
Their kaleidoscopic patterns in the air,
Intent upon an ever-moving now.

I command a world within, active now
As words and symbols weave their spells for me,
But it's tied too tight to the outer air
By sense impressions, and the flying wings
Of every thought are clipped by the bare
Hard knife of fact that around them waves.

It is when my current and the world's waves
Blend in one billow, as they did just now,
That their imbalance is so hard to bear.
There is this difference between things and me:
Things know no pattern; like chaff winnowings
They drift wherever force directs the air.

On wings of wind, the rain-squall drives the waves.
The air above grows dark. Outside me now
The discord lays my limitations bare.

I THANK THAT MAN (for Sylvia Hale)

War's prose had grown in nineteen forty three
Almost anywhere save in my brain
But I in love heard only poetry
And recall my last trip in that train.

There at a station-stop near Exeter
I heard the train-guard's voice, all notes greeting,
As warm as words I knew would come from her
Tomorrow at our bridal meeting.

Over the bridge to Yeovil,
Over the bridge to Yeovil,
Over the bridge to Yeovil town.

I thank that man who in his hearty hail
Intoned his message. Its bell voice was pure.
Too long it slept where other good sounds fail.
Once more in mind it wakens to endure.

"Upon this train you have too long sat still.
Life grows sweet wherever feet move up and down.
The road from here can never grow uphill.
Cross the bridge to Yeovil. You'll find the town.

"Over the bridge to Yeovil,
Over the bridge to Yeovil,
Over the bridge to Yeovil town."

"Though your sex, name and age are different,
The you they are is much too alive to drown.
Where thought and feeling in your words are blent
There comes once more the life of Yeovil town:

"Over the bridge to Yeovil
Over the bridge to Yeovil,
Over the bridge to Yeovil town."

HOW MANY TIMES?

How many times have I seen Vladimir,
An out-fielder whose name is Guerrero,
Propelling his arm like a flying spear
That got to first on time as his quick throw
Coincided with an umpire's strong shout,
"The ball got here first, the runner is out."?

How many times have I seen Guerrero
Steal a base to help with a scoring need
And come out safely with nothing to go
On except for bravado mixed with speed?
More often than not runs of his tally
Continued without ending a rally.

How many times have I seen Vladimir
Imperil health by a play in the field?
Against a pitcher's stuff his way was clear.
He'd take his fullest cuts and never yield;
It really was the thing he was about,
An awesome hit, or more awesome strike-out.

How many times have I seen Guerrero?
And in Winter times the games I recall
Are mighty acts that shift the ebb and flow
Of life with strength enough to make baseball
A duel between two great forces still,
Wild athleticism and too-tame skill.

BANNED WORDS

Life holds more truth in incidental view
Than we know. Poetry is not measured by
Length. What better to exemplify royal
Ignorance and innocence than Marie
Antoinette's quip: "The poor, let them eat cake."
Or Napoleon's, "Where are the pope's guns?"

Dialogues like the German, "*Gott mitt uns*"
And our own reply, "We got mittens, too"
(A homespun pun that makes the clever ache)
Are kin to all our vocabulary.
And, like the song, "Wait till the clouds roll by."
Wash off our squeaky feeling like oiled guns.

Language is kinder than events. Such oil
Can use grey clouds to obscure crushing suns
And swallow them up in our history.
Making us act as if things that we view
Really had been there for us to live by.
We gnawed at life's sawdust, thinking it cake.

Were we to let our minds read gold for cake,
Would such dichotomy be more royal?
It is even more expensive to buy,
Harder, heavier, dead to all reasons.
Aloof to all but self, its useful view
Consists of its dead and dying rarity.

If language were less kind would verity
Not have had more words to describe cake?
Would this add knowledge with a larger view?
If this were so, life would need far less oil
Than is left to multiply our reasons
For what we need who struggle to get by.

How to get by with banned words. I'd ban "buy".
That would give gold no more reality.
The rest of words require fewer reasons.
Take all figurativeness out of "cake".
With this done there'll be no need for "royal";
And what we do then will require no "view".

"Gold", "buy", "oil", "cake", "royal"
Ought not to be used for reasons
In any minds too small to hold a view.

TAO (Revision)

I know five gods by metaphor
That go together 'til time's end.
Charm, Zest, Rhythm, Grace and Glamour.

These wind inside and out each door
Of matter which our senses tend
And living needs no metaphor.

Charm's a pond, quiet at its core.
There reeds of Grace can smoothly bend
To breath-winds where Dawn is Glamour.

In Rhythms which the sunbeams store,
Zest is the magic of the blend.
These five lives make one metaphor

And move as one. They all work for
One God, the Source alike and End.
Charm, Zest, Rhythm, Grace and Glamour.

So sang Lao-Tzu, truth's corridor
Who in one brush-stroke sign did blend
Charm, Zest, Rhythm, Grace and Glamour
With insight more than metaphor.

In the Palliative Ward

In the palliative ward
My wife's attention wavered and
Lost me in her deep fear of death.
Among the other patients one
Was there who was not a stranger.

She had, summers ago, gone to
My children's literature class.
Big and strong, craggy featured,
Almost ugly, but her eyes shone,
Joyed by new available games,
Stories, songs, dances, clever charades,
Whose patterns would create flying
Words of imagination.

I did not even hesitate
But held her, kind to kind, kissing
Her mouth: "Oh!" she gasped, "if ever
Anyone had said, this could be
I would never have thought a thing
As blest as this one could happen
But thank you and God it did."

FARM-BOY

1.

A farm-boy, sun-tanned,
I, all day in a wheat-field,
pulled mustard by hand,

2.

Through the field she walks. . .
Will Mom dream in her sleep-time
that she still picks rocks?

3.

Dad wanted the grain
Safe and dry inside the barn
I just wished for rain.

4.

Caught by Hardy, I
read *Under the Greenwood Tree*
hilariously.

5.

At noon, dry or dew,
I'd pick and stem strawberries.
I counted them, too.

DON JUAN'S LAST TRIUMPH

"Yes, Don Juan, take your time," the devil said.
"Your fate depends on how you answer me."

I take my time and see my life flash by:
A blur of female flesh, plump painted birds
That fell before my male hypnotic gaze
And left their plumage in the trophy rooms
Of memory. I feel the hunting pride,
The surge of power that fed on victory
And gave all games a zest I never queried.
And then I see the Donna Helen's eyes
And hear the "No" come firmly from her lips.
So clear I see that look and hear that voice
I know that his satanic majesty
Who waits in patience for my answer now
Cannot torment me as that woman did.
What's in a look? What's in a word? you say.
Why, if the devil only knew he'd die,
Finding himself and all infernal tricks
Alike redundant. Looks and words are lenses.

That turn a view of heaven into hell.
What did I learn from Donna Helen's then?
The wisdom that the echo learns when first
It is aware the pealing bell exists,
Its small importance in the scheme of things.
She was a woman and not moved by me.
Therefore the force to move lay not in me
But in her self, and then I knew
That this was truth in all my women known:
What moved them was their own hot fires held in
Too long, and not the heat that blazed in me,
And I was dross to feed those hellish flames,
And Helen, being pure, could only burn
On better tinder than the thing I was.
But shall I tell the devil all of this?
He is the Don Juan of souls. It would,
I fear, deflate his thin balloon of pride
To know that power's not in him but in
His victims. 'Twere kind to let him triumph, go
To hell and spare him what I suffer now:
"My lord, I'll say no words in my defense.
I ask no mercy. Work your will on me."

I WILL NOT SAY. . . (Pavane)

I will not say, "Come, play to me."
For with you playing is not play
But a total life-conception
In which all living things are one
That can be neither owned nor given.

Play to yourself, but when you do
In the resultant happening
The selves of you and me are drowned
As two, together, now create
What could be one world orchestra.

Give what music means to music
And you sometimes get a truer sieve
That instantly turns life's chaff
To indescribable wheat
Winnowed by sound-waves into gold.

And make your sense of sound enrich
All silence and its mystery
Till each of us attempts the pitch
Of words that try what can't be said
Because the part cannot be whole.

My ears with notes of gathered gold
And your fingers' bird ecstasy
Are both alive inside the zest
Of patterns which are found to stop.
What can be life can be death, too.

I will not say, "come play with me."
Play to yourself, but when you do,
Give what music means to music
And make your sense of sound enrich
My ears with notes of gathered gold.

AN INTRODUCTION

The least you can do is to start right now
To write a sestina though you have no
Idea as to what its theme will be.
The important thing for you is to make
Your desire tangible by creation
And for the umpteenth time put down a verse.

You respond to life. Get life in your verse.
Imagine a woman before you now,
A fresh avenue for your creation,
One whom you don't know but want to know.
Call her the Muse or Mary Anne but make
Her the centre of what the poem might be.

Muse or maid. This inspirer should not be
Sick or negative, ugly or perverse.
Writers become the objects that they make
When the dead leaves of long ago and now
Fertilize the live tree of yes and no
Bound to be the end of our creation.

Bound to be the end of our creation
The spore, seed, and chrysalis have to be
Still shells for static form. Yes and no
From star to continent – and even verse –
Are all abeyance, and space now
Provides what is, which motion cannot make.

Autumn, anywhere is no time to make
A moving epic on a creation
And such a plastic season is this now
It would be better not to transport "Be"
But simply paint a form in static verse
Leaving unresolved both "Yes" and "No".

Where I am in this poem I do not know
And the road to go by I cannot make.
I've only set some space in a verse
And — worse still — as for complete creation
Of what should be done and what ought to be
I'm almost compelled to say, "I don't know."

Goodbye Muse and Mary Anne. Here I know
Your make is awkward. Now in this long verse
Words put together here can't be creation.

MEMORY

As a boy I had a good memory
But all the world of books that filled my head
Was mixed with the life I saw around me.

Thoughts moved through two lives ambidextrously
But why they did so I often said
Was I used them to support memory.

When I found folk who seldom agree
I kept thoughts to themselves. They were not dead
But never became one with part of me.

The more time passed, the more to disagree
Was anathema to both heart and head
And an impediment to memory.

And that is why if I could I would be
Farmer, pull weeds, use hoe for tongue instead,
And, unopposed inside, be memory.

I don't deny negativity.
Time can have all of it when I'm dead.
As a boy I had a good memory.
As long as I can I'll keep it with me.

DESCENT FROM EDEN

That year the rich banana harvest failed,
When infants tore their mother's milkless dugs
And tasted blood and whined, the wisest apes
Forsook the shelter of the friendly trees,
Leaving their virtue on the leafy limbs.

Stark hunger snapped the tree-forged gentleness
That shuddered at the acrid smell of blood;
The clammy horror of the crawling caves
Fished back the feral lust to feed on flesh
From cold, ancestral seas that knew no sun
Until, sharking in schools again their prey
Through tangled bottoms of a greener sea,
They grew the scourge and terror of the earth.

But still the tree-shaped hands of infants clung
About their mothers' necks, prolonging this,
Like cords umbilical, the natal ties;

And sometimes when the birds of morning sang
A tree would grow inside an apish head
With fruit and innocence among its boughs,
And there the ape would from his fellows climb
To drink the golden waters of the sun
Before returning to his night of blood.

ONCE LONG AGO

Once long ago I thought I owned two worlds.
My dreams were as real in adolescence
And gave to my life what it had not known.
I did bad things there and quite fearfully
Waited long after for consequences
Which never came, but later on when I learned
And grown-ups explained that these things were dreams,
These situations subsided, then stopped.
A fear world left me and never came back.

I think I'm sure now what that loss gave me.
After that, it never took me long to know
That dreams made religions and that worse deeds
Than mine had been in that way created.
This insight helped to win me scholarships.
For what it killed, I as poet pay a price.

DEACON JOHNSON (Revision)

Old Deacon Johnson gave no groundhog board
Upon his farm; he'd root them out by water,
Earth up their holes, and set dogs to the slaughter.
Though he was kindly in both act and word.

It seemed each Spring a flood of rodents poured
Upon his land to sink their shafts in clay,
But no one laughed in meeting when he'd pray,
"No more torment me with thy groundhogs, Lord."

For all of us assembled understood
The deacon's hate of groundhogs and that shot
When he remembered by the Monquart Wood,
Aiming where fog and frost make one spot
He lightly thought to shoot a groundhog dead
And put a bullet through his neighbour's head.

SLEEP, MY WHITE VICTIM

Sleep, my white victim, your perfect control
Lies in your virgin shroud and girdled boss.
Sleep, an impure grossness takes direction's toll
And we lose too soon the road to Paros.

A god's sense doubles the dust on time's bowl
As it eats the heart of a dead tree.
Sleep but, live in your self, breathe from your soul
The newborn notes of your clarity.

These more than survive. Breath and its control
Inside a dispersed trembling universe
Have a keener impact over the whole
Because their own velocity is terse.

For Eighty-Four …

For eighty-four years I could never see a
Lot. My walled eyes were a dark jail
Astigmatism, cataracts, myopia
Always made what I saw seem pale.

Although the world, its old handicaps gone,
Is new glow and sharp clarity,
The change, compared to earlier vision,
Holds more surprise than ecstasy.

Despite these original flaws inside of me
My experience turned out well
And made me believe — farther than I could see —
The mind had good collateral.

TAXIDERMIST

When in my hand ideas expired
Which too long their subsistence drew,
I worked hard after I was tired
To give them shapes like friends I knew.

I painted words that looked like blood
And togged them out in uniforms
As from a life I understood
I humanized quite likely norms.

Now often critics when they read
Let on them their wise wrath rebound:
"Although they move, these do not bleed."
Alas! No poem is holy ground.

TAME GOOSE

Down high ways of heaven wild geese fly.
The tame goose answers with a cry.

Along a ring of palings high
she stretches neck and runs to try
the mocking wings she can't control,

but when the goose-girl brings the rye
she snatches up and gobbles whole
the grain self-nesting in the bowl

nor heeds the whistling winds gone by.

A BALLAD OF ORCHARD EVENING

Out in an orchard evening
They walked without a word,
And apple buds in moonlight
Above them swelled and stirred.

Out in an orchard evening
They walked through apple bowers,
And on them fell the honey
Of gently swaying flowers.

Now back from orchard evening
They come without a word,
But deadly hangs the silence
Between them like a sword.

And lips that kiss at parting
Are now a hail-hard shower
To bruise and shred and mangle
The fragments of a flower.

POET

In me what mind-set
caught in my earliest age
made up a poet?

My voice had no bent
for music and words were my
only instrument

While hither and yon
a million things in the world
cried for expression

Whether badly or good
let other folk than I say
He did what he could.

PAVANE: I WORKED POTATOES

I cut the tubers up all day,
And in each portion left an eye,
Which later on in Summer's heat
Assumed the shapes that all who knew
Could recognize them by their name.

I checked the planter down each row,
Machine-fed in the furrowed space,
And made sure a plant could spring
From the soggy soil of space
That I made free to meet the hoe.

To keep weeds off I'd later till
And cultivate the up-heaped soil
But most attention paid
To keep the team in unison
And every row I planted straight.

In the field I worked potatoes,
Pouring baskets into barrels.
Work was heavy, my back was bent,
But I was paid for doing this
More than for other things I did.

And I was proud of what I did
For payment was not just money
But the relaxing rest of pride
When what I bragged I did was true,
Accepted by all my siblings.

I cut the tubers up all day.
I checked the planter down each row.
To keep weeds off I'd later till.
In the field I worked potatoes
And I was proud of what I did.

WORD-GAME

casual
      as a stone
whips waves
      in mind-sea
that die when it sinks

star
      a fire-hole
            centred
cracks
      rays outward
            fishlines
in the dark
      reverse inward
and catch star

star-fish
      star shrinks
plunges
      huddles in ooze
casual
      like a stone

why do words

        come

where do they

        go

where are they

        when

they are not

INCIDENT

on the gray edge
of consciousness
where vast tides press
the mud's thin ledge

through blue waves of sleep
she swam to me,
Aphrodite
unbound from the deep.

she stabbed at me
without a word
with the white cold sword
of her beauty.

desperate I fled
that hungry strand
to a teacup land
of butter and bread,

where maids are free
of dangerous wish
and only fish
rise from the sea,

but terrible steel
left wounds of fear
on eye, tongue and ear
that will not heal.

No Other Time

No other time was like that time I had.
It was caused by weather that was bad
With fog so thick it blacked my vision's stare
And gave new eyes to skin which everywhere
Paid me a rich return and made me glad.

Feeling insight was a subtle salad,
Blent from skin and air as leaves and sun had
Been. Such mind-chlorophyll existed there
                                No other time.

No other time was like that time I had.
Nature's gift cannot ever be a sad
Happening. However much we compare
Most precious is a rapture which we share
                                No other time.

Their Hands And Ours . . .

Their hands and ours
ape-clenched now hold
not flowers but guns'
lead arguments
whose brimstone smell
is death to right
and wrong, but theirs
are evil, ours good. . .

and this men swear
for truth who would
not dare to say
when two limbs rub
on a sick tree
in a black wind:
"Those must have come
from different seed."

THE TRUE ESSENCES OF GREEN

Water and sun mingled in proportion.
Between them they caught the glint-shine of glass
Softened by the faint blur of almost rain.
Since nuances absorbed one another
The eye, caught by the strength of one colour,
Remembered the world in a short word, green.

Of all the spectrum's hues the one word, green,
Is at best a unit whose distortion
Is necessary. There's not one colour
In our perception, but, clearer than glass,
Function shines; chlorophyll and no other
Builds the bridge-world between sun and rain.

There difference disappears as the brain
Subsumes a hundred hues and calls each green.
As when one vision starves another,
Far perception dwindles thin proportion.
That makes us wonder what we see in glass
Or what it is we can learn by colour.

Even when we close our eyes, the colour
That we want to see, be it sun or rain,
Or something unnoticeable as glass,
Is only what our reflection's green
Has raked up out of our mind's proportion
In motley heaps for time's dust to smother.

As I read I wish that thoughts are other
Than they are and let my eyes see colour
As it is, undone by disproportion
In a war between sharp sun and blurred rain
That blinds me to realities of green
And the particularity of glass.

It is an irony. What is brain's glass?
Words there are at odds with one another
So much that we lose a live world of green
From our vocabulary, lack colour
To feel full energy of sun and rain
That gives the wide world its true proportion.

I know I need another proportion.
I shall not perceive but be sun, rain, glass
Not colours but the true essences of green.

THE GOLDEN FISH

The golden fish beneath the stones
That line the bottom of the lake
Will seldom rise to greet my will
Although I stir the surface up
With hollow reeds of sight and sound,
But when I drown myself in sleep
They dart alive and ripple through
The shining waters of my dream.

The Dragon Tree

Strange-scented birds and song-flowers grow
In the garden where I cannot go,
Where green-trunked trees grey apples hold
And blue fish swim in pools of gold.

And always there a green sun glows
To burn the song of red-leafed rose,
While yellow grasses bend their knees
Before a bluebird-smelling breeze.

Around the garden's circle flies
The dragon-tree to eat the skies
With silver-scented fruit that sings
Hid in the branches of its wings.

That garden now to me is gone
Where sight and sound and sense are one,
But children walk there still before
They eat the dragon's cherished store.

On The Stage Of World Unity

Size does not matter nor does direction,
But when time and distance at last converge
Whether in an atom or a nation
Synchronicity is bound to emerge
Allowing particles to ebb and surge
Somewhere sometime as myriad energy
Living in process or dying to purge.
Bit-parts on the stage of world unity.

Size does not matter nor does direction.
As time always has its eons to splurge.
Life is a game that can never be won.
Its playing field has an elastic verge
That leads it to a dimensional urge
Beyond knowledge into great mystery
Where energies droop and refuse to surge,
Bit-parts on the stage of world unity.

World unity will not ever be won
Till out of it consciousness will emerge
And make with synchronicity one
Great entity. Until then the sad dirge
Of time and space must ebb and pause and surge
Again and pause, and we as pawns must be
Things that coil and recoil with merely urge,
Bit-parts on the stage of world unity.

Go on, Great Prince. Expedite dimension.
Weary of always having energy
The pawns we are grow desperate alone,
Bit-parts on the stage of world unity.

EUPHONY

In music, notes and words both take patterns
Wherein sounds differ, recover, re-differ,
Changing their volume and utterance speed,
Hardness and softness, cadence and euphony.
Inside these, things condense and their parallels
Remind us that all come from the same clones.

Though novelty keeps thoughts from being clones
All things that move possess the same patterns
And from star to atom the parallels
From genesis to coda won't differ.
In birth, growth, decay, death, lie euphony
As energy moves at its required speed.

When energy moves at the right speed
Mind can move difference into clones,
Turn familiarity into euphony,
Fill up missing blanks inside the patterns
In prescribed ways which, before they differ,
Notice corresponding parallels.

A game of snake-and-ladder parallels.
Spite varied bulk and energy, the speed
And lots of things create fates that differ
Underneath the strength of all moving clones.
Painful birth and growth and all the patterns
Where, viewed as one whole, lie euphony.

All elements I view are euphony.
Earth, air, fire, water are my parallels,
And I am a child whose living patterns
Respond to the awesome strength and speed
Of which all animals are living clones,
And the blindness with which their lives differ.

Sweat, blood, sperm, tears are salt. These won't differ
But invoke the sea-waves euphony;
In lust's rage and fire's passion's neat cyclones
The wild thunder-claps invoke parallels
Even the living air revs up its speed
As our lives are joined to dust's dry patterns.

However we differ, ourselves are clones
Who demand more vision of what parallels
Size and speed than is in current euphony.

II

IN MY YOUNG DAYS

In my young days life was not funny.
Day to night, night to day, family
Grew strong roots that held and fed me
Bread that was more like glue than honey.

BIOGRAPHY

Though heat and cold outside my passage went,
Inside were appetite and mystery.
Despite a few hard stones that rocked content
The soil of settlement fed roots in me.

WHAT CAN THE MIND WEAR?

What can the mind wear as a shield
Against the sharp-edged thought it feels?
Some words are calm, but have they healed
The wound each thin-edged scar reveals?

In Life's Wine And Foam

In life's wine and foam
Men worked like bees. Their bodies
Were their honeycomb.

Armageddon

I walk across a land where grass is gone,
Burnt by the fire of a rainless air.
What moves is wind stirring a skeleton
And the dead dust that blows everywhere.

The Dark Road

In the sad north, the dream of Padraig Pearse
Wears its darkest dye, and its hate-love release
Strews blossom and thorn on the brain and heart.

FROM HIS THRONE

From his throne on high
Does the Ruler realize
Ownership must die?

THE STROKE

The whole world spins black.
Will-less, I fall, hugging earth.
And then, ground thumps back.

IN THE DIVINE WORLD

In the divine world
Earth keeps Seed's strength. Self is sin
Unforgiveable.

54

SKY

Sometimes clouds seem white, sometimes dark as dew,
But sky is still a sieve of silent light
That lets both night and day slip through.

ALWAYS THE FULL SHINE

Always the full shine
When moonbeams meet the water
Makes night beautiful . . . .

IN WORLDS WHERE WOE . . .

In worlds where woe and happiness
Alternate from joy to misery
We are symbols of God's largesse
To souls whose worth is yet to be.

AFTER PARADISE

Earth was not appeased in the state of years.
After paradise God's grief was so profound
That fragrant plants and spice became rich tears
And blood-red blossoms filled the desert ground.

PLANTS

Plants age and grow less vernal
Until they droop, pale and bleed.
There's more life inside the kernel
When the fruit is near the seed.

A CONTRETEMPS

I brought her my flute
To make my song be a choir,
But the birds were mute.

ENOUGH

To stop all crying
I shot a mournful curlew –
My wife was dying.

APOLLO AND DIONYSUS

Although Apollo sets with gravity
Each clear task, he's not Dionysus.
Deeper than reason run the tides of life.

ON SHELBY'S ART

When I watch the Cobra's strength out-pour
Tyrannosaurus Rex, I do not trust
Art's design: oil from a dead dinosaur
Poured on a steel canvas that will not rust.

I'm Glad

I'm glad Whatever Is lets these things like
Sounds, words, shapes, colours have a common use.
It stops the urge in me to make them mine.

On Deeds Alone

On deeds alone the scent of death is dark.
Who acts becomes the slave of space and time.
I'll set down words, for thoughts do not grow old.

Trees

Inside all trees what's drawn from light and dark
Is fused to fashion what such beings need . . .
Oh, that I could see men as trees walking!

A Sad Bequest

Despite the carnage of our wars
I don't think that the dinosaurs
Meant all life on this earth to spoil
When they died, leaving mammals oil.

Antaeus

Of ancient warriors strong Antaeus
To me had special worth.
When other heroes leaned on heaven
He drew his strength from earth.

Coolie

Up the slow hill-road
Li struggles on; shade-trees grow
Darker for his load.

TIME AND SPACE

Time and Space are not caught in an embrace
But differ in a trick of imagining.
Death is a dark shadow blotting out Space
Time's God is Light. Both eat everything.

THE MATING

The mating of sugar and salt
Is life that leaps dangerously:
There blood-power hardens to halt
The surge of the wave-verge to be sea.

PSYCHOSOMATIC

Skin saves the body
From all the outer chaos —
Words are the mind's skin.

A COMMENTARY

Women do not hide
Their grief. It springs from their eyes.
Men swallow their tears.

SPEECH OF A NATION

Speech of a nation
Alien to our own cult
Defies translation.

CHINESE HAIKU

Shee Teh, the poet,
laughed seeing the sun-impregnated moon
who dared not show it.

HOUSE AT NIGHT

Whether snap, creak, or silence, in the house
Tonight something uneasy twists and stirs.
If you were here these walls and I could sleep.

WHEN THE BRAIN

When the brain is starved
of any outward hope, love
eats its own heart-flesh.

WITHOUT FULL SYNCHRONICITY

Without full synchronicity
No life on earth can ever thrive
It takes a whole world's energy
To keep each particle alive.

WISH

May a mind like ours
fly over age and fear
and be a meeting of eagles
high up in stainless air.

THE TROUBLE WITH LIGHT

. . . after the after glow
we live with the shadow . . .

REALITIES

we refract our world
through an invisible bowl –
gold-fish do the same . . .

OLD-FASHIONED

Flesh-willed and word-dumb
I could never say to her,
"If you love me, come."

SOLOMON

Proverbs come from the minds' reason
In cold print 'til attention's gone:
From the balm of one green season
The birds taught love to Solomon.

THOUGH POEMS ARE NOT . . .

. . . though poems are not
jewels but polished glass, in
the right light they shine . . .

ADVICE

Don't think fast. Don't move. Stillness is best.
It does not matter whether thought or deed
Are used. There's no variety in speed.
The true cocoon of any change is rest.

LIFE IS . . .

. . . a green blade growing
out of a cleft in the rock,
defying time's cold . . .

INSIDE THE CALM POOL

Inside the calm pool
a dream reflects the amber
of sleeping water.

Miracles

. . . a green leaf clinging
to a Winter bough . . . and you,
incredible love.

Pearls

With nacre does an oyster gild
the hurtful grit beneath its shell;
a poet uses words.

The Dancers

Though of infinity we dancers own
Brief floors of space, thin walls of time, and dance
A spot-dance halted by the caller, Chance,
The music's sweet. We do not dance alone.

It Is Not Enough

It is not enough to feel inside the breast
And deeply sense the past-voice of the skin.
Without mind there can be no love at all.

To Me Joy

To me joy is no net that depends on
My will but on coincidence, a rare
Union of will and the world will draws on.

Each Year

Each year when autumn colours glow, the tree
Puts forth its seeds and after that resigns
To time and chance the manner of their spread.

I Wear My Sun-Cloak

I wear my own sun-cloak against the wind
Of change and take outside loss and gain
As air I shall not miss till breath is gone.

Maulawi

When a sense of divinity
Offers my soul what I need
My fingers woo the maulawi
To coax joy out of the reed.

Condescension

Plants consume their needs.
I, respecting charity,
Cannot call them weeds.

INSIDE, THE STORES . . .

Inside, the stores that sell Sikh women's wear
Are crammed with silk. No artistry is lost.
Don't marvel at the price of beauty there.
Love indeed is clear; some men pay the cost.

WALLED

Walled-state, walled-faith, walled-love, walled-fear —
    we shall
Not go far outside our walls, and the kind
Of selves we are depends on walls' embrace.

THOUGH THORN AND BLOOM

Though thorn and bloom together bless
The air they breathe above,
It is the dew of tenderness
Keeps fresh the rose of love.

Said . . .

Said translator to painter:
"See the world my words mean."
Said painter to translator
"My oils can make it green."

In A World Ruled . . .

In a world ruled by academic arts
I prefer the song the first bards sung.
Although the life-force still beats in our hearts
Other noises have atrophied our tongue.

In A Daisy Field

In a daisy field
one bloom absorbs all others –
your face in a crowd.

Earthquakes In My Brain

Earthquakes in my brain
Messed memory. The wonder
Is that you survived.

What Was Important?

What was important?
I remember touch, but now
I forget her name.

Old Age Is Not Moss

Old age is not moss; there's empathy. When,
Through grief love shines greener than grass or leaf,
Although we pass, our meaning does not end.

71

DISTASTE OF SYMMETRY

Nature's distaste of symmetry
Defeats our human creativity
With its crooked trunk and its crooked root
And the uneven curves of all its fruit.

SINCE ALL THINGS

Since all things in their flow ask us for more
Intensity than we possess, the pitch
Of tunes at last gives back what it began.

ZEN II

Sins matter no more than whims. True knowledge
Is wholly in the process not the pause.
Incarnate Zen is in the word "delicious".

BIRD SONG

Beauty is bird-song,
but once in the air to what
ear does it belong?

DOES YOUR TWO EYES' SHINE

Does your two eyes' shine
express their own new impulse
or imitate mine?

CONTRAST

Machines are cloned; cells
of life-variety are
individuals.

The House Without A Door

I don't know where that house has gone.
Always it said "yes" to my touch.
Always that "yes" pleased me so much
I'd take no other direction.

Watching An Eagle

Watching an eagle
topping the sky
I feel caged.

When In Relief

when in relief, dumb,
my eyes sting salt tears, I ask
from what sea they've come.

Forty-Fives

When I grew up we played at forty-fives
A game perversity gave to circumstance.
It filled up a vacuum in all our lives,
Skill was routine but made our feelings dance.

I Try For Patience

I try for patience in my own heart's core
And make conclusion thus: *What's cool is now;*
What's spun is done; what's to come, chimera.

Amore

The softest of words
and the easiest to say –
How hard to obey!

HOSPITAL, FREDERICTON

I heard a nurse say:
"What a pity these seniors
Don't just pass away."

CONNELL STREET, WOODSTOCK

He told me it was
Sloe gin but it sure acted
Fast enough for me . . .

GESTALT

Since in us sperm and blood and tears
are near enough to ocean's salt;
I think too many sunless years
lost life lived in the world's gestalt.

HATCHING

Before it was hatched
the chick left the egg silent,
completely detached.

DEVIL

Who is a devil?
Each one who likes playing God
Must make God evil.

IN FAITH

In faith bifurcation remains normal –
Religion's rise and fall is everywhere.
Although its speech is too set and formal
Divine absorption is the soul of prayer.

In Easy Morals . . .

In easy morals like American
A greedy company director can
With African sweat-shops, child-bought for gain,
Perform the same role as Saddam Hussein.

Flute

When I at last made breath mine
And the keen flute my fingers trod
My ears discovered truth divine:
The air I breathed came straight from God.

Passion And Love

If passion's cup of carnal ecstasy
Were mixed with love from the heart of a child
Think how fine a drink those draughts then would be
If God had made the mixture less defiled.

EPIGRAM

To write an epigram is tough,
Like drawing landscapes on a pin:
Although the thought is large enough
The altogether-form's too thin.

GRIEF

Grief's a blood-let need.
How can I ever cure it
without veins that bleed?

NO WORD

No word could express
better than her silent nod
the depth of her yes.

When I Close

When I close the taps
spaced-out drops take liberty
on my dream rhythms.

The Best Of Times

After chores were over
There was nothing to do,
Nothing to want,
And nothing to talk about.

Where Metaphor And Action Blend

Once metaphor, now real as actions go:
Who feed the sparrows in a Winter snow
Bring living leaves to grace the frozen trees.

Vincent Van Gogh

fiery lines leap
in the brain and colours burn
when our eyes are closed.

Connemara Sunset

Here in the craggy fells of Connemara
The Seven Pins and the vegetation
Grow black to merge with the giant stones
As red with the blood of a mauve sky's wounds
The sun drops down over Oughterard.

True

true to its own ring
when it's struck a bell will sing
deep out of its wound.

III
Adaptations from the French

MIRABEAU'S BRIDGE

(Guillaume Apollinaire)

Under Mirabeau's Bridge Seine waters flow
      And our loves
Must one remember where they go
Enjoyment has always come after woe.

The Darkness is nearing, time rings its bell
The days go along and in them I dwell

With hands inside hands, face to face let's stay
      While under
Our land bridge we'll let our looks stray
On the eternal wave of everyday.

The Darkness is nearing, time rings its bell
The days go along and in them I dwell,

Like soft water flowing is how love went
      Love will leave
Because life is gentle, like Lent,
And because hope is always violent.

The Darkness is nearing, time rings its bell
The days go along and in them I dwell

Through day and through night moves Life's slow train
        Neither part-time
Nor the lovers come back again
Under the Mirabeau Bridge still flows the Seine.

The Darkness is nearing, time rings its bell
The days go along and in them I dwell,

Like water flowing is how Love went
        Love will leave
Because Life is gentle, like Lent,
And because Hope is always violent.

The Darkness is nearing, time rings its bell
The days go along and in them I dwell.

DUSK

(Réjane Baezner)

The lake's taffeta lasted till sunset
That shone in our eyes a blue-green desire.
Dusk smoothed everything like a warm fire.
The fine ring of the moon was quite silver yet.
So fine a gleam (bubble it might be called)
That died in the sky with sunlight's ashes
Where we saw over-hanging the gashes
The huge fire of dusk with force unequalled.

This my heart found as night discreetly caught
A faint fringe of blue over a child's cot.

SHELL-FISH

(Réjane Baezner)

The lot shell-fish command
Ends as a one-day shove
On barren burning sand.
It's like the end of love.

Now that time is at hand;
Alas! the wind-blown spray
Jingles over the strand.
Love soon is dried away.

Shell-fish, the air's wonder
Can tear colour apart
And ear's tear not thunder
Be the tale of a heart.

NOCTURNE

(Jules Breton)

The night still mingles with waves pallidly.
A star is born. Through its reflected fog
In the quiet pond lurks a bull-frog
The fields, the waves, lack all formality.

With closed calyxes the flowers are lazy.
Foreseen through the air that's making it damp
The sickle-sky rests in its corner ramp.
The mist under its pearl-tears digs deeply.

Too drowsy the constellations engage,
And the birds, blurred under their black foliage
Taste, beak under wing, a peaceful rest there.

In the great slumber of earth and being.
For a long time now the dreamy toads sing
Their sad and soft flutes to the lonely air.

AUTUMN'S RETURN
(Jules Breton)

The harvest is done and packs the hay-lofts.
Fields are bare, woodlands are red, and sorb-trees
Are vibrating in fog like living embers;
Toward their grape's red coral, the thrushes,
Heaving weak cries, are arriving in swarms
While the sparrows, always prompt to steal,
Are coming back to thieve in the courts where
The straw's pallor is joined to the sadness
That tips a white sun in a soft pale sky
While forgotten gods are waking in us.

FAITH-LINE
(René Char)

The kindness of stars is to ask us to speak, to show
us that we are not alone, that the dawn is a
roof and my flame your two hands.

89

WOMAN

(Cécile Cloutier)

In a web
Catastrophe
A queen bee
Pregnant with honey
Is still.

Tomorrow
A civilization
Of wings
In the sun.

AT THE DIZZY END

(Cécile Cloutier)

At the dizzy end
Of the spiral
And of the fall
Experience is calmed
By a ring

At the end of two rings
A chain.

THE LAST POEM
(Robert Desnos)

Nothing remains for me but you.
I've walked so much, I've talked so much;
So much I've loved your shadow touch
That nothing else I know is true.

I'm shadow among shadows rife.
A hundred times more you I welcome.
I am the shadow that will come
And return in your sun-lit life.

ON AN ANIMAL LADDER
(Paul Eluard)

I

A bull like a huge cog-wheel
Far from sand, far from water
While inside its scarlet eye
A great club is taking root

A bull falling on the ground
Like an arch or like a spear
Cleaving man in his milieu
And creating in his blood

The foundations of the sun

II

Fine weather is the wind's prey
Grass is the prey of good beasts

Between the horns of the bull
Gushed out the spring of its blood

The foamed-out spring was living
Fists shaken over treasure

And the light without passing
Which never recognized death

III

Beneath the bull's open horns
Feather and lead in accord
Sunlight held out a mirror
To the dark torch-lights of fear

Glory a bull leaving grass
Pumping its huge harmony
While its flesh is a battle
Won in advance by its heart.

PROLOGUE

(Léonard Forest)

we are clothed in an immense nakedness
smiling and untouched, modesty so ill-bred
that there the true sweet joys of summer's dress
mean to the soul nothing but scorn and dread.

mere spatterings of snow our passions are;
on fields hardened by our teeming desire
so young consumed, the sumptuous jar
of our failed loves takes place without fire.

for neither life nor love nor summers burn;
we have love only for harvest's delay.
the green fruits of absence die out in turn
in the dark grass of hope that drifts away.

from now on we'll wear a black joy that gets
in by stealth, lulling to sleep bye and bye.
under pleasant shrouds, in hidden closets
of our regrets we are dressed up to die.

COUNTER-EXILE

(Léonard Forest)

we parted like those who will learn rapture
and we who yet were young were as young then:
round, free, standing timber, wood to endure
through all the hardships of the world of men

above all, hearing you, each day learning
stillness from the tides in the fall
living to smile at your restless burning
loving you, but saying nothing at all.

our trips expressed exotic exile, though
no ship so well has round its headlands sped
nor built again the nautical zero
of lost weights, design of joys forfeited

the weight of god plus time's weight, this ballast
threw us to destruction. then from the sea
but far, far off, an east wind came at last
to tell us what we had formerly

above all, hearing you, each day learning
stillness from the tides in the fall,
living to smile at your restless burning
loving you, but saying nothing at all

all our wanderings are fine and sapient,
all our evasions push against the flow,
and i think at last that tomorrow's bent
stirs a mere tenderness sighted long ago

above all, hearing you, each day learning
stillness from the tides in the fall,
living to smile at your restless burning,
loving you, but saying nothing at all.

THE FOREST

(Louis Fréchette)

Oaks on the thoughtful brow, pine's mysteries,
Old trunks leaning over furious sources
In your eternal and lofty fancy
As you sometimes dream of what used to be
When the savage echo in Canadian oases
Knew but the sound of Indian voices
Who, underneath your branches' wide shelter,
Mingled war-cries with the fall's roared welter?

Under the starred sky, where winds' aerial whims
Balance in darkness your long frantic limbs,
Did you dream of the gold days when our sires
Tamed barbarities without making repairs
As from one seed, heart filled with but one vow,
They posted your shade, crying, "God wills it now!"
Clearing the woodland, creating new homes,
And re-united under night's vast domes,
Still obsessed by their need now to re-praise,
In their bugles blowing zestful new days?

No doubt a story from another age:
You have survived alone a shipwreck's rage
When men are over other men interred
And, despite time which treats little ones hard,
Your foliage which the years' blurs left too long,
On all sky-winds sings but your epic song!

THE BIRD OF FOAM

(Louis Guillaume)

The bird of foam and salt which ties
to it parenthetic power,
the rock, the sea, and the great skies,
the bird which never never dies
and opens up its whitest flower—
when the bright sun awakes once more
that bird goes to sleep on the shore.

And it is by heat of embers
that each of its dreams remembers
so it bends, crossing vision's will,
evading all sails recumbent,
dodging itself and keeping still,
looking again for that lost isle
there where its dead selves always smile.

The bird of the snow, winds and rain
is resting upon my window.
It must labour on earth again
in the ripe clay of all mornings,
reaping for itself each day's dawn
in grains of light as they come on
with the mighty thrusts of its wings.

SECULAR FLOWER

(José-Maria de Heredia)

On the charred ash of the last gradient
Where volcanic dust tarried formally
The grain which wind on big Gualitari
Sowed, seeds, is frail plant, follows its bent.

It grows tall. Where its roots take their descent
Its trunk, drinking dark flame, is fed in shade
And a hundred year's sums have ripeness made
On its huge button that is torn and rent.

At last in burning air that it still holds,
Under the huge pistil it blew away
As its stamen thrust out its pollen gold

And the huge aloes of the scarlet bloom
Ignored the hymen — whose dream gave love room
For a century — flowered only one day.

MAGIC AIR

(Pierre Jean Jouve)

High on the same roof breathes a magic air,
Curling the waves and woods continually;
A breath amid the tragic forms so rare,
Made one through the sky's deep intensity.

Air washes free
Lungs and heat and flesh or, all the same waves woes,
Chagrin, hope and melancholy.
Absent heat and hay air re-clothes;

Erasing hates from love — magically —
Of woodlands, like pride in prologues green,
It engenders a truly great scene,
Making true theatre in our eternity.

PLANT-CALM

(Jean Lahor)

The sage loves the peace and sweetness of plants,
Their female looks and their serenity,
And the sage loves, too, the beasts' nonchalance
Who sleep by him in immobility.

Tonight when he gives in to life's weight and size
So much he's weary of thought and dreams, too,
That he goes to woods where sadness envies
The flowers that are awake to love's calm view.

For God seems to have built inside our skulls
Just sterile torments and toil that is vain,
Resuming here for plants and animals
Passivity, calm and absence from pain.

LIFE AND DEATH

(Gatien Lapointe)

Heart with no country nor comrade
Living embers in my fist

O violent voyage of one word!

I have learned nothing,
I've understood only this tree
Which grips itself to the earth

And which says NO.

METHODS

(Raymond Guy LeBlanc)

To the colourless smell of a candelabra
A flame spreads in the dawn
To the concern of black hillocks
Humming the arches

Windows weep and a man with a grin
Determines to gallop his eyes
Through the smoke

The enchantment of rockets meeting a wall
And somewhere in the spread
Stories watered down to a spark

And all that
Because the candles continue to sing
The reputations of barefooted monks
And the adventure of mankind in space.

YES, I AM WEARY . . .

(Jean Moréas)

Of you, Paris, and of Autumn, I'm weary
    Now that I without avail
Can see the pliant earth and frothy sea
    In the breath of a brisk gale.

Now what filter ever for what grief
    Will be worth all your rancours?
November, you know it's your dead leaf
    Grows my heart its live odours.

I hear my lips, voice Cyrenean,
    Stress more than a song commands
And what light-beams from Springs Castalian
    Spill over out of my hands.

You have jaded me, Muses, like a drowned
    And too rich and hot liqueur,
And my soul is under a lovely mound,
    Lying where your flowers were.

THIS EVE, DAYLIGHT WILL LAST LONG. . .
(Anna de Noailles)

This eve daylight will last long. Time's thinning.
Reports of bitter day are put to flight
And the trees, surprised not to see the night,
Stay awake in the white snow, reflecting . . .

The horse-chestnuts, heavy with their gold cells,
Seem to spread their odours everywhere.
We do not dare to walk or shift the air
For fear of disturbing their tender smells.

The far-off rumbles return to abodes . . .
The dust which a small breeze upward has moved,
Leaving the live tree, weary she's reclothed,
Comes back softly again to the calm roads.

Every day we see, straight forward and plain,
That road so simple and often pursued,
But now something has changed us more than mood;
We shall never have that night's soul again.

HUMAN MATTER
(Claude Péloquin)

a tree like everything is itself
belongs to no one
possession is a window-dressing complex

it's the thing that lets us talk about it
as if we saved it.

ISN'T THERE ANY BETTER WAY TO HAVE PEACE?
(Claude Péloquin)

. . . a toureg with a skin disease
and allergic to wool
is dressed in wool
for better fighting
for better hating . . .

MOMENTS

(Claude Péloquin)

there is no difference in time
between the driver's moment when he lovingly parks
his new truck
in a rear unit of a Val D'Or motel one afternoon
in the course of a trip
between that peasant woman's moment as she passes by
holding a live rabbit by the hind legs chatting in Catalan
near a truck parked on the dizzy height of the Pyrenees
between that Italian pope's moment in the morning
as he fondles
his chalice like a truck fender

they are all three
whoever they are and they must not die any more and
they must be able
to take the time to make the moment last
so that the long road the stew and the guilt may
be consumed.

GLUM SONNET
(Jean Richepin)

It rains and the north wind's strong breath
Sinks all things. Firmament breaks down.
A good time for its dream to drown,
Under the black ocean of death.

Let's drown it, a dog-gnawing breath,
Hup! Stout rock and short cord release
And at last we shall find our peace,
The amoral slumber of death.

But we were weary and we chose
Not suicide but to linger;
We read; we yawn; make poetry;

Listen; then drink casually
While the rain with its green finger
Beats out a charge on the windows.

REFOUNDED

(Arthur Rimbaud)

Refinding is done!
What? Eternity
Is the light of sun
That mingles with sea.

Your soul on its own
Clings to your desire
Despite dark alone
And your day on fire.

Self-free from gages
Of human party
And common rages!
Your flight is hearty.

Never providence,
No *orietur*,
Science and patience,
The torture is sure.

Tomorrow, no more
Satin's beauty
And there your ardour
Has become duty.

It is refounded!
What? Eternity,
Sunshine compounded
With sheen of the sea.

POEM

(Francis Viélé-Griffin)

At first I ran; speed paid youth's cost;
After I sat down and withdrew:
The day was soft and the compost
Was moist and warm; your lips were, too.

My walk was both heavy and slow
In the lightness of love's lithe strength.
What shall I say that folk don't know?
I have marched for a whole day's length.

And then just as I left the road,
There came a darkness suddenly:
I laughed at the horror you showed
But night contained, corseting me.

Forty-Four Haikus by Jocelyne Villeneuve

The Spider's Toil

Its silver threads drew
out of the sunshine and dew
Threads new…Threads broken…

Mime

Slow the road awaits
Under the sleeping birches.
The sun imitates.

The Magic Wand

Broom upon the stoop . . .
A joyful dust is sweeping
Up all the sun's rays.

Good-Day

lily, sunflower fawn
as they ape pretty curtsies —
greetings from fresh dawn.

Evasion

Crickets are singing . . .
I am caught in the stillness
that surrounds the earth.

A Drowning Death

The moon was bathing . . .
a great cloud passed by, drowning
her in its shadow.

Confusion

A menagerie . . .
dark is sweeping light away,
as the star-dust falls.

Slow Down

Eternity was
cradled in roses, and I
saw nothing at all.

Metronome

Tick tock tick tock toe
too impatient hastes the flow
of time in my life.

Mistaken Vision

Not flowers fly there
over ends of velvet air
but bright butterflies.

In the Garden

See the child there sway —
Fingers steal the thought away.
It's gone with the wind.

After

A sad departure . . .
Over water a fish hawk
trails a longer voice.

Hair-Cut

Behold the swallows
clip and reclip the blue sky
with their scissor blows.

Returning

Voices of children
animate the far meadows.
House is quiet then.

Juxtaposition

Poem in the grass —
Spider looks for words to make
Her an alias.

Mirror

Sky in the water . . .
The fish are sneaking in now
underneath the clouds.

Rest

A moonlight growing . . .
hung upon the highest branch
of a sleeping pine.

Owl

An owl in the night
with two eye-like sunflowers
can discover light.

Slumber

A ring of moonlight
spreads itself inside of me . . .
then sleeps happily.

Invocation

A disturbing night . . .
the shrill cry of the osprey
remembers her breath.

Hide-And-Seek

Rushing to pond's edge
I attempt to meet the moon
that's already gone.

Lovers Under Rain

Hand in hand they go —
gold threads that tie together
both earth and heaven.

Preserves

Scarlet raspberries . . .
A red odour born out of
syruped sunshine.

Destiny

They talk of flowers
I have not seen . . . of summers
that no longer come.

Shadow-Mania

The dog my fingers
designed on the wall is shrewd —
A barking shadow.

Nocturnal

Heaven's balcony
from which one by one Night hurls
all its shooting stars.

Reveries

Gay from bloom . . . to bloom . . .
to bloom again butterfly
my frivolous thoughts.

Nostalgia

The netted curtain
that flaps in the wind . . . warm rain . . .
The past, sweet again.

Land Surveyor

Thousands of gold canes
Measure the time as it flies
along the gutter

Wheelbarrow

The nocturnal rain . . .
Summer in the wheelbarrow
Burdened with blue sky.

Indecision

On what soil to dance?
Anywhere where the sunlight
Unveils a shadow.

Lacerations

Noonday has rung . . .
At the same time, grasshoppers
are scraping the heat.

Evening Performance

We need not cry "Hark!"
Joy is like a pin's shadow
lost in total dark.

Occupation

The furrows stretch out
as they excavate cradles
for a Summer night.

Solar Clock

Does a shadow's length
indicate the time of day
or the heart's real strength?

Open Air Quadrilles

Elevating trills
that lift silent marshes up
in star-dancing quadrilles.

Reflexes

The salt taste begins
on water, the silty froth
of our origins.

Grandfather

He packed his pipe tight —
The blackbird tidies his nest —
Come and go for both.

The Dictionary

a, b, c, d, e . . .
Hundreds of words hidden in
a single iris . . .

Error

Spider on ceiling? —
No: a black encrusted task . . .
drawing out its thread.

Synchronous

The day comes around —
On fire, water puts it out
With but little sound.

The Honeysuckle

Fine perfumery
is weaving its leaves and flowers
to infinity

Memory

I hear the thrush sing —
Behind me; forgotten notes
Of another Spring.

Moments of Grace

Rose wheat-stalks, and then . . .
Flesh of an eaten melon —
So twilight meals end.

I Do Not Worship Centuries

I do not worship centuries
In which time dwindles to a breath
So slight a few enormous trees
Sigh in their sleep unwaked by death.

Here life and death are not by will
But chance. Time-worships not for these.
In the long run things grow or kill
Dependent on inanities.

THE LOVES OF THE EYE

caught in light's shimmering net
out of sky's fabled water
from salmon flesh of morning
to the starfish-schools of night
the loves of the eye

so adjusted is their flow
in the ways wherein I move
that I bless the wantonness
with which such things come and go,
beauties I can't own.

MIRRORS MAKE MAGIC

(from Phantastes[1], *by George MacDonald)*

"Mirrors make magic . . .
A room becomes poetry
Perceived through glass."

---

[1] First published 1858